How to Write a Perfect Essay:

The 10 Step Essay Guide for GCSE, A Level and University Students

Jonty Purvis

About the Author

My name is Jonty Purvis and I am a Cambridge
Geography graduate. Up until I was 15 years old, I
performed fairly average at school. I often received poor
marks, and never truly realised my potential. However,
all this changed when I started my GCSEs. Whilst looking

at past papers, I realised a trend throughout all the essay subjects. Certain aspects existed in every mark scheme, allowing me to make a blueprint for the 'perfect' essay. This turned everything around. Despite being nowhere near as naturally 'smart' as many of my classmates, I began to outperform all of them.

A few years later, I found myself studying at arguably the top university in the world. Here I was surrounded by true geniuses, who were many times smarter than I was and put in many more hours of work every day. However, even at Cambridge, I managed to outscore most of my cohort in my essays.

After graduating, I started my own private tuition business (Revision Hive) based in London. Here I teach my various essay writing techniques to GCSE, A Level, and University students in a number of subjects such as French, History, English, and Geography. We have recently expanded, and now offer tuition in every major subject, including Science and Maths.

We aim to teach every student how to use the mark scheme and various writing techniques to ensure they get the best possible grades in their work. Most importantly, we are all young, friendly, and relatable. All of the tutors at Revision Hive are either current Uni students or recent graduates, and we understand that a relaxed and fun approach to tuition, combined with learning the vital strategies and techniques, is the perfect way to teach our students.

If you are interested in getting in touch with me or booking private tuition lessons (for online or in person), visit The Revision Hive website at:

www.revisionhive.com

Table of Contents:

Foreword

This book will explain the '10 stage' process of writing the perfect essay. It is aimed primarily at GCSE, A Level, and University students looking to improve their essay writing skills. Whilst these skills can be used in any subject to improve the quality of your answers, it is particularly useful for students studying English, History, Geography, Business, Sociology, and French/Spanish.

Each of the first 10 chapters of this book will relate to a different part of the 10 stage process to essay writing. For a quick reminder of the 10 stages, see the Summary in Chapter 11. For examples of essays which use this technique, see Chapter 12.

I will use the metaphor of baking a cake in order for students to easily visualise the essay writing process. The most important thing, however, is to practice. You won't win The Great British Bake-Off if you've never baked a cake!

Again, if you wish to contact me about private tuition or any other questions, please visit my website:

www.revisionhive.com

Chapter 1: The Mark Scheme

There are 2 things needed in order to write a good essay. The first, of course, is hard work. If you are unwilling to research properly (or revise properly for exam essays), then you will never do well. This will be discussed in more detail in Chapter 2.

The second, and most important, is the mark scheme. If you do not know what the examiner is looking for, then how can you fully realise your potential? It is like baking a cake without a recipe. If I were to tell you to bake me a Victoria Sponge birthday cake, then would you know exactly what to do? Sure, you might be able to make an average cake with some of the right ingredients, taste, and texture, but it almost certainly wouldn't be perfect. The same thing happens with an essay. If you do not know the requirements needed to gain full marks, then it is almost impossible for you to score well. Mark schemes are crucial!

The first and most important thing you can do before starting any essay is to look at the mark scheme. For both coursework and exam essays, this can always be found online on the exam board website. Once located, you must look at the marking 'levels' or 'criteria' required to reach the top marks. This can often be worded quite confusingly, but usually there are key phrases that appear in the mark scheme which must be remembered. This includes words like "evaluation", "strengths and weaknesses" or "casestudy". These words are going to be critical for anyone wanting to score well on an essay.

Also, for many GCSE and A Level subjects, mark schemes are split up into various 'Assessment Objectives' or 'AOs'. A deep understanding of these assessment objectives is extremely important. Whilst these AOs vary depending on exam board and subject, they usually have some similarities.

For Geography, the AOs can often be broken down into something like this:

AO1 – Facts

AO2 – Evaluation and answering the question

For subjects such as English, the AOs can be more complicated:

AO1 – Quotes and Answering Question

AO2 – Language analysis

AO3 – Context

However, these Assessment Objectives vary significantly between subjects and exam boards, and it is important that you look at your specific exam board website and make your own notes on exactly what the Assessment Objectives are.

Even if there are no AOs, such as when writing university essays, there is still usually a marking criteria or 'rubric' you can access to find out exactly what is required in order to achieve the highest marks.

Once the AOs have been identified, it is important to delve deeper into the mark scheme in order to understand how much of each AO is needed to achieve full marks in the essay. If the Assessment Objectives are the 'ingredients' needed for the cake, then the rest of the mark scheme can be seen as the exact amount of each ingredient that is required. This is equally as crucial for achieving successful marks.

If we return back to the Geography example, the mark scheme will often state how, for a 12 mark question, there are 6 marks for AO1 (facts) and 6 marks for AO2 (evaluations and answering the question). This is incredibly useful information which needs to be remembered. It will allow any student to look at their own work and think:

"OK, I have a lot of facts, so I will probably get 6/6 marks for AO1. However, I only answered the question at the end of the essay, meaning my AO2 marks could be 1/6."

When you can think like this, you are already getting close to writing the perfect essay. This student has obviously worked hard to learn lots of facts, so it would be a shame to only get 7/12. All they have to do now is practice answering and evaluating the question throughout the essay, rather than the end, and they will soon be getting 12/12!

When it comes to a subject like English, this becomes even more important. If a student has a knowledge of the Assessment Objectives, they can analyse exactly where they are losing marks, and how these problems can be fixed. Let us say there is a 25 mark English question, and the mark scheme breaks down the marks into 10 marks AO1 (quotes and question), 10 marks AO2 (language analysis), and 5 marks AO3 (context). The student can then think:

"OK, I have learnt quite a few quotes, and I am not bad at answering the question, meaning I will likely get 8/10 for AO1. However, I only analysed the language from 1 of my quotes, meaning I may only get 2/10 for

AO2. I also completely forgot about context, meaning AO3 will be 0/5".

This student has worked out, due to their knowledge of the Assessment Objectives, that they will get only 10/25 for the essay, despite the fact they learnt lots of quotes. This would be a disaster for such a knowledgeable student, but it can easily be rectified. If the student simply analysed 2 or 3 more of their quotes, they would move their AO2 from 2/10 to 8/10. As for their context, if they added a short piece into every paragraph, they could easily get 5/5. Suddenly, they have gone from 10/25 to 21/25, which is almost certainly a Grade 9 / A*.

The point of these example is to show how critical an understanding of the mark scheme and assessment objectives is for achieving the best marks. Without the ingredients or the recipe, your Victoria Sponge cake will likely be a disaster. Once you have these guidelines, then you will make a much better cake, even if you are not a natural chef (or essay writer!).

So please, before you do anything else, find the marking criteria for your subjects and make notes on the Assessment Objectives or requirements needed. You won't regret it!

Chapter 2: Preparation

Any good chef will tell you that preparation is key for success. Without the right equipment, your cake will never be made properly. The same can be seen when writing essays. Mastering the Assessment Objectives and Mark Scheme are critical, but there is no point in doing this if you have not put in the preparation work beforehand. Without preparation, you will have poor facts and content. Without content, your essay will suck!

The quality of facts required completely depends on the level you are at. If at GCSE, names and dates may be sufficient. At A Level, a detailed understanding of context, along with quotes from critics or authors, would be a good idea. At university, a variety of detailed references and sources must be implemented. Whatever the case, a good essay requires good facts.

Think about these 3 answers from a GCSE History exam:

1. **The Treaty of Versailles was a disaster for Germany, and they suffered economically and socially as a result.**

2. The Treaty of Versailles was a disaster for Germany. Economically, £6.6 billion in reparations was required to be paid, and this had many social implications.
3. The Treaty of Versailles, signed on 28th June 1919, was a complete disaster for Germany. The economic implications were most devastating, with £6.6 billion forced to be paid to the Allies. This caused social issues, with anger at the Weimar government eventually leading to the Kapp Putsch in March 1920.

The first answer would likely score a 1 out of 5. The second answer has a good economic fact, and may well score 3. The last answer, however, has 3 dates and various other facts, and would easily score a 5. What is important here is to realise that all of these students knew the same thing about the Weimar government. The only difference was that Student 3 had put in the work to revise and learn some key dates and facts, putting their answer at a much higher level than the others.

Obviously, facts are crucial to success in an essay. In coursework, these facts do not even have to be learned, you just have to do the research and insert them into your work. For exams, however, revision must be done to ensure facts are remembered accurately.

So how should you revise facts? Revision guides, whilst not enough on their own, are certainly a good tool to start with. To bake the perfect cake, a 'Cooking for Beginners' book may not take you all the way, but it will certainly help you get started. The same can be seen with revision guides. CGP books in the UK are an excellent resource, particularly for GCSEs. Even digital resources such as SparkNotes or BBC Bitesize, whilst not perfect, are a good place to fill in knowledge gaps.

But in the end, the only thing needed for learning facts is YOUR hard work. Whether it comes from writing out pages of notes, jotting key facts on revision cards, or simply underlining the textbook, a detailed knowledge of the subject is critical to any essay.

'Detailed' is the important word here. For English, you need to learn direct quotes and techniques, for History a variety of dates, and for Geography an array of casestudy facts and figures. Once these details are remembered, the preparation is complete, and the cake is ready to be baked.

Chapter 3: The Plan

Before baking a cake, should you go straight into it, and start randomly throwing ingredients into the bowl? Or should you quickly plan the basics of how you are going to make it?

Planning an essay is critical to success. My teachers always told me to spend 5-10 minutes planning an essay. Whilst this can be good, I personally think this is too long. I HATE planning, it is boring and it wastes time, but it is still crucial for the success of an essay. Therefore, I like to keep my plans quick and basic.

Here is a good, quick plan for a Geography essay:

'Trans-national Corporations (TNCs) have an overall positive impact on the country they are operating. To what extent do you agree?'

Intro – Agree to a small extent

Para 1 – Agree, economic benefits (Vietnam casestudy)

Para 2 – Agree, social benefits (Nigeria casestudy)

Para 3 – Disagree, social disadvantages (Nigeria negatives casestudy)

Para 4 – Disagree, environmental disadvantages (Mexico casestudy)

This took less than 5 minutes, but is the perfect plan to move forward with. It states the line of argument, it lays out the structure of the essay (2 agree paragraphs and 2 disagree paragraphs), and it outlines which casestudy will be used in each paragraph.

This should be done for any essay, whether it is coursework or in an exam. Without a plan, the essay will likely have a poor structure, fail to answer the question, and may miss out crucial details.

Some people prefer more detailed plans which discuss exactly what will be talked about in each paragraph. For English, this often involves writing down the main quotes that will be used in each paragraph. This is also a good strategy, particularly for a subject which requires quotes, as it ensures you will not end up re-using quotes in different paragraphs. Whatever your plan looks like, the most important thing is that it has a line of argument.

My Geography plan, for example, states my argument in the introduction, and carries on my balanced argument throughout the plan. If you cannot follow a line of argument in the plan, then how can you follow it in the actual essay?

Here is a BAD example of a plan for the same question:

Para 1 – Economic

Para 2 – Social

Para 3 – Social

Para 4 – Environmental

This is not a good plan. Whilst it contains similar information to the first plan, it does not really layout an argument, and only mentions one word on what the paragraph is about. Paragraph 2 and 3 are both on social factors, but it is unclear whether these are positive or negative, and there is no mention of any casestudy that will be used.

Whilst plans should be short and sweet, if it is too short it will lack the information necessary for a good plan, and may confuse your line of argument when it comes to the essay.

When I bake a cake, I often get halfway through and realise that I do not have the right equipment (such as a mixing bowl), or I do not have an ingredient (such as vanilla extract). This slows the process down as I have to go out and buy the right ingredients, or I may even go without the ingredient completely, meaning the cake is not nearly as tasty.

Poor planning leads to poor execution, and this is why every essay must be planned (for around 5 minutes) before it is written.

Chapter 4: Answering the Question

The first thing you should always do in an essay, at least at some point in the introduction, is answer the question. Whilst this seems so obvious, it is also something missing from so many people's work. We are trying to make a Victoria Sponge cake, so if you make a chocolate cake, or just a plain cake that has no real flavour, then the cake has failed. The same can be seen with essays: Answering the wrong question, or not directly answering any question at all, will result in a poor-quality essay.

The need to DIRECTLY answer the question cannot be underestimated. If the question is "to what extent do you agree?", then you must say exactly how far you agree. There are various ways to answer this type of question, but a simple and effective way is to either say "I agree to large extent" (if you strongly agree), "I agree to a small extent" (if you feel there are 2 sides to the argument), or "I disagree to a large extent" (if you disagree). Many essays require two sides to an argument, and this makes the "I agree to a small extent" answer a very effective technique for ensuring you answer the question whilst leaving room to argue both sides of the argument.

Answering the question, however, should not just be done in the introduction. It should be done EVERYWHERE. At the start of each paragraph, for example the question must be directly referred to. Let us look at an example:

'How far do you agree that Hitler had widespread popularity in Germany in the 1930s?'

Introduction: "I agree, to a small extent, that Hitler had widespread popularity in Germany..."

Para 1: "One reason that shows how Hitler had widespread popularity in Germany is..."

Para 2: "Another reasons that suggests how hugely popular Hitler was in Germany is..."

Para 3: "However, it could be argued Hitler did not have widespread popularity in Germany because of..."

As you see here, the start of each paragraph refers directly to the question. This may sound a bit silly, and when at university you do not have to be quite as repetitive (although you should still be regularly answering the question!). However, this is extremely necessary for both GCSE and A Level essays. In fact, you do not only have to refer to the question at the start of the paragraph, but also at the end:

Para 1 End: "All of this suggests how Hitler certainly had widespread popularity in Germany in the 1930s.

Para 2 End: "Evidently, Hitler was an extremely popular figure in Germany in the 1930s".

Para 3 End: "This shows how, despite his popularity amongst many, Hitler did not have complete widespread popularity in the 1930s.

With so many marks available for answering the question in every essay, it is vital to directly refer to the question both at the start and at the end of every essay.

In fact, you should also probably refer to the question halfway through the paragraph as well. This is particularly the case if you are making more than one point / using more than one piece of evidence in the same paragraph. Even if you are not, you should probably refer to the question throughout the paragraph, at least indirectly, to remind the examiner you are certainly answering the question.

As will be discussed later in this book, the question must not only be answered, but also analysed, evaluated, and debated, in order to achieve the highest possible marks. But for now, the most important thing to remember is that you must directly refer to the question throughout the essay. If this is done, then even if the content of the essay is bad, you are still likely to receive a decent mark due to the fact you have answered the question.

As my old teacher used to tell me: "The Title is Vital". If you ignore the details of the title/question, you can never answer it effectively, and you will never receive a good mark as a result.

Chapter 5: Structure

Whilst structure has already been partially covered in the last 2 chapters, it is important that you fully understand how to implement a good structure to your essay.

If you do not follow the cake recipe, and just throw all the ingredients in the bowl together, it will never be as successful as if you follow the recipe in detail, adding each ingredient exactly when it is required.

Whilst the structure of an essay varies hugely depending on the subject and exam board, the basics of the structure generally remain the same.

For my GCSEs, A Levels, and University essays, my structure always looked something like this:

- **Introduction**
- **Para 1**
- **Para 2**
- **Para 3**
- **Para 4**
- **Conclusion**

Now let us go into more detail. If it is an essay where 2 sides of the argument are required (which is most essays), then the structure should look like this:

- **Introduction – Agree to a small extent**
- **Para 1 – Agree**
- **Para 2 – Agree**
- **Para 3 – Disagree**
- **Para 4 – Disagree**
- **Conclusion – Balanced argument**

Similarly, if it is still a question for an essay where 2 sides of the argument are required, but I want to mostly agree with the question, then the structure should look something like this:

- **Introduction – Agree to a large extent**
- **Para 1 – Agree**
- **Para 2 – Agree**
- **Para 3 – Agree**
- **Para 4 – Some may disagree because...**
- **Conclusion – Agree**

Almost every essay possible can implement one of these 3 structures. The first is more basic, and is usually for an essay which does not require an evaluation of 2 sides of an argument. The second and third, however, are a great way to deliver two sides of the argument: The second gives a very balanced structure, whereas the third is more 1 sided but still offers both viewpoints.

You may have noticed that each of these structures includes 4 paragraphs in the body of the essay. Whilst this can change depending on subject, 4 paragraphs is probably the best option. 3 paragraphs are possible if very detailed, or if the question has few marks, and 5 paragraphs are also possible if you can find enough to talk about. Some people like to do 6 or 7 paragraphs, and whilst this is fine, it usually means the paragraphs may not be detailed enough to gain full marks.

Another very important aspect of structure that people tend to struggle with is the fact that each paragraph must be about a DIFFERENT point. There are so many essays where students will have 2 paragraphs that are extremely similar, and this simply wastes time and confuses the examiner. Each paragraph must have its own 'theme' that relates to the question. Let us look back at the Geography essay plan from Chapter 3:

'Trans-national Corporations (TNCs) have an overall positive impact on the country they are operating in. To what extent do you agree?'

Intro – Agree to a small extent

Para 1 – Agree, economic benefits (Vietnam casestudy)

Para 2 – Agree, social benefits (Nigeria casestudy)

Para 3 – Disagree, social disadvantages (Nigeria negatives casestudy)

Para 4 – Disagree, environmental disadvantages (Mexico casestudy)

Here, each paragraph has its own clear theme in relation to the question. Paragraph 1 is talking about economic benefits of TNCs, paragraph 2 discusses social benefits, paragraph 3 discusses social disadvantages, and paragraph 4 analyses the environment. These are 4 extremely clear points that easily fit into 4 different paragraphs.

Now let us look at a more difficult example from an English essay:

'Explain how far you think Shakespeare presents Lady Macbeth as a powerful woman'.

Intro – Agree to a great extent

Para 1 – Agree, her dominance over her husband

Para 2 – Agree, her 'masculine' / unisex traits

Para 3 – Agree, her powerful language and imagery

Para 4 – Disagree, her eventual breakdown

For more complex essays, particularly in English, it is harder to make sure each paragraph is completely different. However, it is crucial that each paragraph is different enough and is based around a different overall point. Here, paragraph 1 focuses on Lady Macbeth's relationship with her husband, paragraph 2 focuses on her 'masculine' traits, such as her want to be 'unsexed', paragraph 3 focuses on the powerful and violent language she uses, and paragraph 4 suggests how she is not powerful in the end as she seemingly has a breakdown. Each paragraph directly answers the question, but each paragraph has a different overall theme, and this is key for writing a good essay.

Overall, the structure of an essay is perhaps the hardest part to get right, but it is also the aspect of an essay that will ensure you can get a good mark. A good structure will ensure you answer the question fully, cover a range of relevant content, and present your argument in an informative way.

I think the most important part of this Chapter to remember is the way in which the 'to what extent' or 'how far do you agree' or 'evaluate' questions are structured. For these questions, I always try to get at least one paragraph offering a different side to the argument. Even if you agree to a great extent with the question, you should still include a paragraph that offers an alternate view in order to achieve full marks. A good way to do this is to begin your final paragraph by using phrasing such as: "However, some people argue that...". This wording allows you to give multiple sides to an argument without contradicting yourself. It also allows you to gain evaluation marks (something which will be discussed later). At the end of this paragraph, after outlining the alternative view, you can then critique this view and say why it is wrong and why your argument is correct. This is more advanced, but should certainly be done at A Level and university level to achieve the very top marks.

Chapter 6: The Introduction

If the very start of the cake making process goes wrong, such as mixing together the incorrect amount of butter and sugar, then the whole cake will fail. Introductions, like the start of a cake, form the basis for the entire essay, and it is critical that the introduction is excellent. In fact, the introduction is the first thing an examiner will read in the essay, and they will immediately start to form an opinion about what mark to give the essay based purely on this opening section.

If I read a good introduction, then I am already thinking that this essay will receive an A or A*. Even if the rest of the essay is terrible, it might only fall down 1 grade to a B. For a terrible essay, a B is a very good mark! However, if the introduction is terrible, then I am already thinking the essay will receive a D or a C. Even if the rest of the essay is amazing, it may only go up 1 or 2 grades to a B. For an amazing essay, a B is not a good mark!

Basically, the introduction can put the examiner in a good mood and help set you out for success. Moreover, an introduction is the perfect place to answer the question, something which rewards lots of marks in every single essay.

As stated before, the first thing that should be done in an essay is answering the question. This should be done AT LEAST ONCE in the introduction. Let us look at the Lady Macbeth question again:

'Explain how far you think Shakespeare presents Lady Macbeth as a powerful woman'.

The first sentence could look something like this:

Lady Macbeth is presented as an extremely powerful woman by Shakespeare in the play.

This is very simple to do, but also very effective, as it immediately answers the question and shows the examiner you have understood what is required.

In terms of the rest of the introduction, this completely depends on the subject and whether it is a GCSE / A Level / university essay. For GCSE, a 1 or 2 sentence introduction is usually enough, whereas higher levels often require more detail.

GCSE Introduction:

Lady Macbeth is presented as an extremely powerful woman by Shakespeare in the play. Through her relationship with her husband, as well as her compelling language, she is portrayed in a powerful manner throughout the play.

A Level Introduction:

'Lady Macbeth is presented as an extremely powerful woman by Shakespeare in the play. Whilst her power fades towards the end, she is portrayed for the most part as a dominant woman, both in terms of the language she uses and in her relationship with her husband. Women in Jacobean England were often seen as subservient to their husbands due to the patriarchal society in which they lived. Shakespeare effectively uses Lady Macbeth to reverse this stereotype, showing her as powerful and domineering woman throughout the play'.

For GCSE, once you have answered the question in the introduction, only 1 more sentence is probably required. This sentence can layout some of your paragraphs, just to give the examiner an idea of what you are going to argue. By saying: "Through her relationship with her husband as well as her compelling language", it suggests to the examiner that my essay will discuss her relationship with Macbeth and her powerful language, which it will! This is an easy strategy for writing a short, simple, and successful introduction at GCSE.

For A Level and beyond, more than 2 simple sentences are usually required. A good strategy to follow is to use some background context to introduce the question. Since the question here is about Lady Macbeth, an excellent piece of context is the way women were seen and treated at the time. Adding this in will not only give you 'context marks', but will also set the scene for the examiner and show that you have a detailed knowledge of the topics.

The next page offers a '4 part' structure for completing the perfect introduction. Whilst some subjects will not require each of these parts to be implemented, it is a good idea to try and include as many of these aspects as possible in order to complete the best possible introduction.

A detailed introduction should have 4 main parts:

1. Answer the question

Lady Macbeth is presented as an extremely powerful woman by Shakespeare in the play.

2. Discuss what you will talk about / your different paragraphs

Whilst her power fades towards the end, she is portrayed for the most part as a dominant woman, both in terms of the language she uses and in her relationship with her husband.

3. Give some background

Women in Jacobean England were often seen as subservient to their husbands due to the patriarchal society in which they lived.

4. Say something clever to answer question again.

Shakespeare effectively uses Lady Macbeth to reverse this stereotype, showing her as powerful and domineering woman throughout the play'.

Particularly for A Level and at university, this style of introduction is critical for ensuring the examiner is impressed right from the start, and gives them confidence that you will be achieving a great mark.

A common question is whether or not the introduction should layout EXACTLY what the essay will argue. For example:

"This essay will first discuss Lady Macbeth's relationship with her husband. It will then discuss her powerful language, before finally analysing her fall from power at the end of the play".

Some examiners like this and others do not. I think if you follow the 4-part structure then the second sentence should cover some of your arguments without saying EXACTLY what the essay will do. This is a better strategy than the above introduction, as it sounds more natural and less formulaic. However, as long as the main parts of the introduction are covered, it should not really matter how the paragraph discussion is presented, as they both cover the same points.

Chapter 7: The Body

It is difficult to give specific advice about the body of an essay because it completely depends on the type of question and subject. A chocolate cake, for example, will contain some different ingredients to a Victoria Sponge. However, in whatever subject you are doing, each of your paragraphs in the body of your essay should follow a similar format:

1. **Introduce the paragraph using words of the question.**
2. **Main part of paragraph with different facts, remember mark scheme and making sure everything is included.**
3. **End the paragraph by again using the words of question.**

For example, if we were to answer a Geography question about volcanoes, the structure would look something like this:

'How far can earthquakes be seen to have a more devastating impact than volcanoes?'

1. One way in which earthquakes can be seen to have a more devastating impact than volcanoes is through their significant social effects.

Here I have introduced the paragraph (about social effects of earthquakes) and have used the words of the question (more devastating impact).

2. Firstly, they often cause tragic levels of death and injury, due to both their primary and secondary impacts. During the Haiti Earthquake of 2010, the 7.0 magnitude earthquake killed up to 220,000 people, either by the initial shock or in the aftermath due to disease and starvation which swept through Port-Au-Prince. Whilst volcanoes can often cause casualties, the numbers are generally nowhere near as devastating, usually due to a relatively small area being affected when compared to earthquakes.

Here I have provided relevant facts and figures to support the theme of the paragraph (earthquakes have bigger social impacts than volcanoes).

3. **This evidence suggests how earthquakes can be seen, to a great extent, to have a more devastating impact than volcanoes.**

Here I have finished the paragraph by summarising it and relating it to the words of the question.

Put 1, 2, and 3 together and it makes an excellent first paragraph for the essay. For the second paragraph, it is good to make it follow on from the previous paragraph to help the essay flow. For example:

As well as their social effects, earthquakes can also be seen as more devastating than volcanoes due to their economic impacts.

This nicely follows on from the 'social' paragraph and continues my line of argument into a new 'economic' paragraph.

A similar thing can also be done when looking at the other side of the question (in a 2-sided argument). For this essay, it could look something like this:

However, the devastation caused by volcanoes cannot be ignored. In fact, volcanoes are often much more devastating than earthquakes in terms of their environmental impact.

By using a phrase such as 'however', it immediately shows the examiner that we are now looking at a different side to the argument. For example, we are now saying how, whilst the social and economic impacts of earthquakes are greater than volcanoes, the environmental impact of volcanoes is more severe. The 'however' thus avoids any confusion as to what exactly you are arguing.

Whilst this seems basic and a little repetitive, it is crucial for both GCSE and A Level essays to show the examiner or marker that you are fully answering the question and all of your argument is clear and relevant. For university students, the answers do not need to be so formulaic, and there should be more room for innovative answers. However, even at University it is crucial that the body of the essay remains relevant to the question, so many of these strategies should still be implemented to ensure the best possible marks.

Chapter 8: Evaluation

Evaluation involves a deep analysis of the question and its topics. Whilst this should still be done at GCSE level, it is much more important for A Level and university students to ensure the highest grades.

Evaluation can be seen as going 'above and beyond' a simple answer in order to really impress the examiner with your critical argument. It should involve offering multiple different sides to an argument, looking at the strengths and weaknesses of each argument, and even critiquing the question or the wording of the question to offer innovative arguments or viewpoints.

There are many ways to include evaluation in your essay, some of which we have already covered. If a question asks 'how far' or 'to what extent', and you have a debate in your essay about exactly how far or to what extent you agree, then this is good evaluation. Even if the question does not ask this, there is still room for good evaluation. For example:

"Evaluate the success of an urban transport scheme you have studied"

This question still gives you good room for debate and evaluation. If your answers only looks at the success of the transport scheme, then this is not evaluation. However, if your answer looks at the successes and failures of the scheme, or even better examines to WHOM the scheme was successful, then that is excellent evaluation. For example:

The transport scheme in London has been primarily successful. The congestion charge zone, charging a fee for travelling in central London between 7am and 6pm, has helped reduce traffic and environmental degradation. Moreover, the 'Bike sharing scheme' has helped to provide easy and affordable transport around London, whilst again reducing issues of pollution in the City. However, the scheme was not entirely successful. Elderly people and people with disabilities who may not be able to easily travel by public transport have been negatively affected by these changes. They are being charged substantial fees for continuing to drive around London, and have seen little benefit from the new system. Therefore, whilst the transport scheme has been mostly successful, it has certainly not been a success for everyone.

This is a great piece of GCSE evaluation. Whilst the first half of the answer is an average response, the second half helps to go 'above and beyond' by really evaluating the impacts of the scheme for different people. By saying it is 'mostly' successful, but not entirely, this is excellent evaluation for the examiner to easily give marks for.

Another example can be seen through the earthquake question from the last chapter:

How far can earthquakes be seen to have a more devastating impact than volcanoes?'

Overall, whilst earthquakes certainly have a more devastating impact socially and economically, they have less of an environmental impact than volcanoes. In the short term, at least, this makes earthquakes more devastating overall than volcanoes. However, in the future, with the increasingly dangerous impacts of climate change, volcanoes could likely be seen as a more devastating. Moreover, the threat of a supervolcano is much greater than the threat of any potential earthquake, and a supervolcano eruption

would have a devastating impact that could affect the entire world for decades. Therefore, whilst earthquakes do have a more devastating impact than volcanoes currently, this could well change in the future.

This is a great piece of evaluation as it really analyses the words of the question. It also looks at the short vs long term, which is another great technique for getting some evaluation marks. Particularly for A Level and university students, the ability to take a word from the question, such as 'devastating', and really analyse what it means and its different interpretations, is something which is likely going to see you receive the very highest marks in any exam or coursework.

Chapter 9: The Conclusion

Finally, you've finished the basics of the cake, and now all you need is the decoration. Something perfect to finish it off. This is the conclusion.

Conclusions should always have 3 parts:

1. Answer the question
2. Summarise the arguments
3. SSS (Say Something Smart)

Much like in the opening for every paragraph of the essay, the opening for the conclusion should also aim to thoroughly answer the question. Let us look at the conclusion to a History question:

"Luck was the major cause of Hitler's rise to power. How far do you agree?"

1. **In conclusion, I agree to a small extent that Hitler's rise to power was mostly due to luck.**
2. **The economic crisis in Germany, combined with public anger against the Weimar government,**

were crucial in allowing Hitler to flourish. However, Hitler's compelling speeches and successful tactical manoeuvres suggest that it was not entirely due to luck.

3. Overall, Hitler's rise to power involved a combination of both luck and his influential persona. Whilst luck probably was the major cause, it was certainly not the only reason. Leaders throughout history have often made use of fortunate situations to gain support or influence, and the successful way in which Hitler used Germany's dire position to his advantage certainly cannot be ignored.

This conclusion uses the 3 part formula stated above. Firstly, it answers the question, saying how far I agree. Secondly, it offers a brief overview of the key arguments of the essay (economic crisis, anger at Weimar, Hitler's speeches, Hitler's tactics). Lastly, it 'says something smart' in relation to the question. In fact, it evaluates the question using the techniques from the last chapter. It suggests how there is not one clear cause of Hitler's rise to power. The fact that he was lucky was certainly important, but the way Hitler used this luck in his favour was equally as crucial for his rise to power. This evaluation would be well received by an examiner, and the fact it is the final part of the essay leaves the examiner with a positive view of the essay as a whole.

Moreover, one thing which has not been discussed in this book is timing. This is because timing is sometimes not an issue (such as for coursework), and even if it is there is little that can be done to make sure of good timing apart from good planning, lots of practice, and a precise writing style.

However, when it comes to conclusions, time is often running out. It may therefore not be possible to write more than one or two sentences. If this is the case, then concentrate solely on answering the question. Summarising the argument is not entirely necessary, and neither is SSS. As long as the question is fully answered, then that will be sufficient if timing is an issue.

Chapter 10: Checking Over

Once the cake has been completed, it just needs a few last touches: The icing on the cake and the cherry on top. Smartening up an essay is of great importance, particularly if you have written it quickly in an exam.

When checking over an essay, there are two important things to ensure. First is the quality of spelling, punctuation, and grammar. Whilst not crucial, poor grammar can certainly have an impact, and if it affects the examiner's ability to easily read your work then it may well harm your mark. The correct placement of commas is often an easy way to resolve this, but all grammar should be checked as the essay is read through.

The second and most important aspect of reading back over an essay is making sure all the bases are covered. This includes everything discussed in this book, such as covering the Assessment Objectives, answering the question throughout, and making sure to have good evaluation. Once this is all completed, the essay is finished. A piece of cake!

Chapter 11: The 10 Stage Summary

In summary, there are 10 stages to crafting an essay, and all of these should be covered to ensure the best possible marks.

1. Know the mark scheme and AOs.
2. Know the relevant facts and knowledge.
3. Do a good plan beforehand.
4. Answer the question throughout.
5. Have a good structure.
6. Do the '4 part' introduction.
7. Ensure the body of the essay is relevant.
8. Include excellent evaluation.
9. Do the '3 part' conclusion.
10. Check over your work.

The final thing to do is practice. Learning how to write the perfect essay will not happen overnight, and only with thorough practice will you ensure you can write an essay to impress any examiner or marker.

Chapter 12: Examples

To finish this book, I will include a couple of example essays that follow the 10 stage model. One of these essays is a GCSE English Literature essay that I wrote recently in a tutoring lesson with one of my students (you may recall it from Chapter 6), and will therefore be slightly less detailed than what would be needed for A Level (although I think it would still score fairly well at A level!). The other essay is a Geography essay I wrote whilst studying at university, and will therefore be far more detailed than what would be needed for GCSE or A Level. However, whilst very different pieces of work, both of these essays contain the exact same techniques that have been covered in this book.

Try to find every time that I either answer the question, give some facts/quotes, or give some evaluation. You should find this at least once in every paragraph, if not much more! Also look at the structure of the essay, including the quality of the introduction and conclusion, and see if I have followed my own 3 and 4 part formulas.

Essay 1 - GCSE English Essay:

This essay follows the GCSE mark scheme that includes AO1 marks for quotes and answering the question, AO2 marks for language, and some AO3 marks for context.

'Explain how far you think Shakespeare presents Lady Macbeth as a powerful woman'

Lady Macbeth is presented, to a great extent, as an extremely powerful woman by Shakespeare in the play. Whilst her power fades towards the end, she is portrayed for the most part as a dominant woman, both in terms of the language she uses and in her relationship with her husband. Women in Jacobean England were often seen as subservient to their husbands due to the patriarchal society in which they lived. Shakespeare effectively uses Lady Macbeth to reverse this stereotype, showing her as a powerful and domineering woman throughout the play.

Firstly, Lady Macbeth is presented as a powerful woman through her relationship with her husband. Throughout most of the play, she is seen as the more dominant figure in the relationship, often doubting Macbeths ambition. For example, the soliloquy of "Yet do I fear thy nature / It is too full o' th' milk of human kindness" suggests how she feels Macbeth is too "kind" to do what is necessary to become King. She even uses rather feminine imagery such as "milk" to describe him. To be denounced by your own wife as too feminine would have been seen as highly insulting and embarrassing in 17th Century England, but lady Macbeth does not appear to be concerned. Her evidently dominant relationship with her husband is certainly one way in which Lady Macbeth is presented as a powerful woman in the play.

Furthermore, Lady Macbeth can be seen as a powerful woman in the play due to her constant desire to be 'removed' from the classical feminine stereotype. She states one of the most famous lines of the play, "Unsex me here", and this is used effectively by Shakespeare to show Lady Macbeth's desire to subvert the feminine norms of Jacobean England, and be reborn simply as a being of "direst cruelty!". Interestingly, it could be argued Lady Macbeth is not at all being a 'powerful woman', as she is attempting to remove herself from gendered discourse entirely. Rather than a powerful woman, some may argue Lady Macbeth is attempting to transform herself into a powerful man. A feminist argument could critique this as damaging gender equality, as only by removing herself from femininity can Lady Macbeth be seen as powerful. However, I would argue that Lady Macbeth is simply revolting against the gendered stereotypes of the time, and her desire to be "unsexed" does indeed promote her as a powerful woman in the play.

As well as through her actions, Lady Macbeth can also be seen as an extremely powerful woman in the play through the language that she uses. She regularly uses imperative language to assert her control of the situation, such as "give me the daggers" or "come, give me your hand". The Jacobean audience watching the play would have been surprised and potentially shocked by how commanding Lady Macbeth is with her use of language. She often regularly uses hyperbolic and 'ungodly' phrases to make her point, such as "Come, thick night / And pall thee in the dunnest smoke of hell". The language she uses arguably makes her seem more like a 'King' than her husband, and certainly evokes her image as a powerful woman in the play.

However, although Lady Macbeth can evidently be seen as a powerful woman, this is not the case throughout the entirety of the play. In fact, towards the end of the play Lady Macbeth becomes deranged, and may have even taken her own life. She is overcome with guilt, with phrases such as "will these hands ne'er be clean?" and "who would have thought the old man to have had so much blood in him?". The rhetorical questions used here magnify her madness, presenting her as a crazed woman muttering to herself and question her own actions. This is in stark contrast to her actions throughout the first half of the play, and suggests how Shakespeare does not want her to be presented to a full extent as an entirely powerful woman. However, no character is given complete power or control for the entire play, and Lady Macbeth can still be seen as overall powerful woman when compared to the rest of the characters.

In conclusion, Shakespeare has evidently presented Lady Macbeth as a powerful woman in the play. Through her relationship with her husband, the way in which she removes herself from feminine stereotypes, and the language that she uses, Shakespeare presents Lady Macbeth as indicative of a strong modern woman, rather than a woman from the patriarchal 17th Century. Despite the fact that she seemingly descends into madness towards the end of the play, this does not take away from the fact that she is primarily presented as a powerful woman throughout most of the play, and a woman who could very much be considered 'ahead of her time'.

Essay 2 - University Geography Essay:

This essay received the top mark in the cohort at Cambridge (1st**). However, I have cut it in half as it is otherwise too long. I have included it here to show how university essays are less 'structured' and repetitive than GCSE and A Levels, and allow more room for innovation. For example, the start of each paragraph does not quite as explicitly use the words of the question. However, you will see that even in this essay, the question is referred to multiple times in a paragraph, evaluation has been done consistently, and my introduction and conclusions still follow the same structure we have looked at it this book.

'To what extent have digital tools such as Sat Nav and Google Earth rendered traditional maps and globes obsolete?'

Since the Enlightenment, efforts have been made to produce more 'realistic', systematic, and universal maps (Stoddart, 1986). This has only been magnified in the modern era, with digital tools such as Google Earth producing a singular, geospatial version of the world accessed by millions of people (Crampton, 2010). This has led to an inevitable decline in paper map usage, with companies such as Rand McNally and the California State Automobile Association greatly reducing production of traditional maps (McKinney, 2010). Overall, tools such as GPS and GIS are not only allowing users constant access to precise digital maps, but also the ability to create their own. This has been called a 'new cartography' (Olson, 1997). However, as this essay will argue, such digital tools have certainly not rendered traditional maps and globes obsolete. 'Traditional', for the sake of this essay, shall be defined as any non-digitalised map or globe. The use of traditional maps may well be changing due to the 'new cartography' of the digital age, yet they still have a variety of uses, and there has arguably been a 'renaissance' of traditional map and globe consumption in recent years (Hurst and Clough, 2013). This essay will state how traditional maps and globes have historical, artistic, and practical value, before analysing the problems with digital cartographic tools, and suggesting a possible future for traditional maps.

Perhaps the most important aspect of traditional maps and globes is their historical and sociocultural value. Foucault's critique of knowledge can be applied to cartography, with maps helping to legitimise and promote global discourses throughout history (Foucault, 1973; Harley, 1988; Ehrenberg, 1987). Since the cultural turn in the 1970s, academics in the social sciences have focused on the power relations behind knowledge, and the idea of multiple truths. The map is a perfect embodiment of these ideals, and academics of History, Geography, Sociology, and even Politics have begun to study traditional maps and globes in order to help in "understanding a prevalent idea", particularly oriental and geopolitical discourses (Brotton, 2012, p. 438). For example, the Hereford *Mappa Mundi*, from the 13th Century, depicts the thinking of the medieval church at the time, with Jerusalem at the centre of the world, and biblical events annotated around the map (see Fig. 1) (Hereford Cathedral, 2016). Similarly the *Kangnido* map offers a view of the world from 15th Century Korea (see Fig. 2). With a huge China dominating the centre, and a tiny Europe and Africa to the West, it is a marked difference to the medieval European maps, which would often ignore the geographic size of Asia (Brotton, 2012). These traditional maps are of great historical importance, showing the power of cartographic representation as a way of building hierarchical order and discourses in our world (Harley, 1989). Such discourses and power relations of traditional 'paper' maps can also be seen in the modern era. The images depicted on the back cover of the 'Official State Highway Map 1978' of North Carolina are interesting (see Fig. 3). An oryx (resident in the state zoo) is shown, along with a ski lift and a Cherokee woman making jewellery (Wood and Fels, 1986). This is evidently a promotional advert for North Carolina, but also depicts the power of the state over its territory. Domination over nature can be seen via the oryx and the ski lift, whilst the Cherokee woman arguably represents an oriental, hierarchical scaling in the state, placing the woman on the same level as the 'nature' which the state claims to dominate (Harley, 1989). Evidently the study of paper maps, with their variety of annotations and images, can help trace social mechanisms and discourses, helping to enrich our historical, geopolitical, and postcolonial understandings of society.

Interestingly, various studies have shown how paper maps still have a practical use for directional and planning purposes, and are often more popular than digital tools for doing this (Hurst and Clough, 2013). There are fears that GPS may be leading to "geographic illiteracy and [diminishing] our sense of direction" due to the fact that they often only show direct routes and immediate surroundings, rather than paper maps which show the 'big picture' (Mahaney, 2014; McKinney, 2010). In fact, it has been shown that people using paper maps rather than GPS devices make fewer errors, and arrive at their destination more quickly (Ishikawa et al., 2008). Moreover, paper maps are preferred to and used more frequently than GPS when the user is on foot, and many people have less confidence and capability using GPS than traditional paper maps (Hurst and Clough, 2013). Confidence and capability are a particular issue, especially amongst the elderly population, many of whom are still not online or have very minimal digital literacy (Ofcom, 2015; Milosz and Milosz, 2013). For this reason alone, it is extremely unlikely that digital tools which replace traditional maps in the near future. Furthermore, numerous studies have suggested how paper is still crucial to our daily lives as it is easy to share, annotate, and has a flexible spatial layout (O'Hara and Sellen, 1997). The fact that paper consumption has remained relatively stable, despite the evolution of digital technologies, suggests that paper map usage may see similar trends (Guimbretiere, 2003). Overall, paper maps evidently still have significant practical advantages for a number of people, and their accessibility and low cost will do more than enough to "keep the format alive" in the future (Hurst and Clough, 2013, p. 59).

Advocates of digital tools often suggest how they offer an objective, universal, and 'correct' view of the world, "without the inevitable subjective bias and prejudice of the cartographer" (Brotton, 2012, p. 407). However, this is certainly not the case, with tools such as GIS equally as subjective as traditional maps (Pickles, 1995). Such maps are products of modern culture, no better or more accurate than maps of previous generations, just different in style and presentation (Crampton, 2003). Kitchin and Dodge (2007) provide an interesting example of 'John Doe's' map of population change in Ireland, to show how even apparently objective maps "emerge through a set of iterative and citational practices" (p.337) (see Fig. 7). 'John Doe' may have used GIS to produce his map, but this in itself is a standardised technique, presented in a way that has been shaped by a scientific culture of conventions, rules, and standards. Just as medieval conventions may have produced an aesthetically pleasing, religion orientated map, the modern cartographic community expect statistically correct data presented onto an accurate geographical background. However, the individual still has a number of choices to make when creating his GIS map. For example, whichever technique he chose to categorise his data (fixed intervals, mean standard deviation, percentiles), as well as which colour model to use (RGB, HLS, HVC) would each have produced a different map (Kitchin and Dodge, 2007). Whilst these individual decisions may seem small, the sum of them creates a certain spatial representation, certainly not an objective or universal one. Presuming the objectivity of digital maps is an increasingly significant issue, particularly as one company, Google, currently holds an almost total "monopoly" over the geographical information that is in the public domain (Brotton, 2012, p. 436). Even in vast geographical databases such as Google Earth, many subjective decisions are made about how the map will be presented, which facts/areas to include, and what the map is seeking to communicate (Monmonier, 1991). Digital tools cannot therefore claim to be 'superior' over traditional maps, only that they present their data differently.

Overall digital tools have not made traditional maps and globes obsolete, and likely never will. Whilst the nature of traditional maps and globes may have changed from simple directional usage to having a more historical, sociocultural, and aesthetic value, this has in no way rendered them useless. On the contrary, the obvious subjective nature of traditional maps is proving crucial to academics in an era of deconstruction and 'multiple truths', helping them trace social and political ideologies over time (Foucault, 1973). Conversely, digital tools often operate "behind a mask of seemingly neutral science" (Harley, 1989, p.7). This is a problem, as believing in the absolute objectivity of tools such as Google Earth could lead to a form of 'cyber-imperialism' of knowledge (Crampton, 2010; Brotton, 2012). Every culture has a specific way of viewing and representing its world through maps, and we must ensure that digital tools do not conform to a purely Westernised notion of cartography. Despite how 'realistic' these tools may be, "there is simply no such thing as an accurate map of the world, and there never will be" (Brotton, 2012, p.445). Moreover, as shown in the aforementioned studies and examples, traditional maps and globes are seeing increased popularity for both their aesthetic and practical values. Whilst digital tools certainly provide real time, extremely accurate, and highly detailed geographic data, it has failed to destroy society's love for the simple paper map.

Made in the USA
Las Vegas, NV
16 February 2022

44000754R00038